Songs of Kindness

By

Joanna M. Lawrie

For Zina Morrison, who always believed.

I've always written poetry. As a child, as a way to explore the world and rhymes; as a teenager, filled with angst and rage (not much has changed there); to adulthood, trying to find new ways of expression and conveying the beauty and terrors and anger at the world around me.

This book is definitely more the first.

I believe strongly in kindness. In the willingness and determination to be kind to everyone—including myself. Too many people confuse kindness with niceness, believing that if you value kindness you should roll over and let anyone have their way no matter the detriment to you.

This is not kindness.

This is being too nice.

Kindness takes courage. Kindness is saying in a world which is all too often unkind that no, I will not sit back and watch others—or myself—be hurt. I will not sit back and be a passive observer when there is cruelty or injustice. Kindness is as political as it is a behaviour.

Kindness, sometimes, is fighting back.

Does this seem like a contradiction? It isn't. To tolerate intolerance leads to a world where intolerance wins. Always be courageous, if you can. Always stand up, if you can. And above all...

Always, always, be kind.

I love your outfit! I get told on a semi-
regular basis when I wear my brightest
colors, standing out in the sea of gray
which makes up the cold office in which
I spend my days. *You look so bright, especially
since it's cloudy out!* I smile as though it was
my intention all along, to brighten up
a miserable day. It wasn't—I just thought
it would look pretty and this was what
was clean. But then again, what a wonderful
idea—to dress for and as the weather you
wish was happening outside. Be the kindness
you want to see in the world, and the
weather you want to see too.

On a gray and cloudy-skied day, be
your own sunshine.

       i can always smell it in the air, though no one ever
                 believes it, the crispness
stinging the back of my nostrils as i breathe deeply of it,
                       ice and cinnamon
                   hot apple pie
       leaves turning from green to
       red to
       gold
    falling in thick carpets which seem
        to give off their own light on overcast days
                 even
when dulled and sodden with rainwater
              glowing to guide the ghosts
       which permeate the air around
    and perhaps—
       perhaps—
          it is them that chill me, bundled
in thick coats and gloves and scarves and
         hats with pompoms on top
      like ones
     i wore
  as a child, in my
innocence.
perhaps,

                     (perhaps, i
                     whisper to
                     myself)

perhaps
it is why the season speaks to me, memories
      of childhood strong and vibrant and always,
        always,
            at the tip of my brain
        (hallowee-o, shake your feathers)
    (cakes shaped like cat faces)
     (dooking with forks and faces in cold water
       until fingers crinkled)
(parties and costumes
       and
    oh. everything.)
           hallows and hellos and halls await
   and i...
   and i...
       i greet autumn with an open heart.

you are not
the people you know or see on the street,
random passers-by or close bosom buddies who boo
when you say you've had a bad day, who buy
you drinks or a rainbow slinky to make you
smile

you are not
the number on your scales, the food you eat
despite the old adage, or the games you play all night
when you can't sleep, to drive away the demons
that haunt you at three a.m. despite your
xanax

you are not
the meds you take every morning, to keep you
sane and happy and healthy, to stop the pain
in your head and heart and also your stomach
because gastritis is no joke when it wakes you
up

you are not
your taste in music or tv or movies even though
some people make this their entire personality
(you know the type), not the way you dance
either alone or out in a club, on a dancefloor, in your
head

you are not
the pets you own, the stuff you own, the style
in which you decorate your home: bright colors
or neutral, cheaply mismatching or expensive in
the best and worst possible ways, cluttered or
neat

you are not
your mental illness, your illness, your neurotypicality
or neurodiversity, whatever drives you or keeps you
from achieving your full potential, whatever
that means anyway because what you do is always
enough

you are not
and yet you are all of these things—the true sum
of every multitude contained within you but
somehow more that even all of that combined. You
contain a whole universe inside you, child of the
world,

and you will
always be important and vital and safe in the
knowledge that your existence means something:
you matter.
you matter.
you matter.

she always seemed ancient, even though she couldn't have been
as old as all that, hair still raven black with one single streak of grey,
swept up in the same style every day. she was a force, always
for good, knowing our strengths and weaknesses individually
for every pupil in her care. in

such a small village school, perhaps that wasn't so difficult, and yet
it still seems like such a feat that she cared enough to really see
each of us as individuals. i remember that she knew i loved to learn,
would make sure i had enough to keep me interested. her kindness
shone through, even when angry. the

other children would disrupt for disruption's sake, angry that this
teacher made them learn, made them concentrate on two-times-two
is four and the plural of sheep is sheep, but i only disrupted by
accident. her laugh, when she laughed, was deep and infectious—i
remember the pheasant incident. she

was reading us our friday chapter of *danny, the champion of the world*,
and the scene with the pheasants flying out of the pram made her
laugh so hard she almost fell off the upright piano where she sat,
cackling and slapping her leg with mirth. we had to draw a scene
from the book when she finished it. we

most of us drew that one. i think it was the first time i had seen a teacher
—a person in authority—as a human person rather than *teacher*, that
any of us had. that was why it was funny—the scene was fine but what
made us laugh was seeing her doubled over with tears of joy streaming
down a prematurely wrinkled face. i

will always remember her that way

and the way her eyes twinkled when she spoke to me

and 'you're not a lark, you're a hoot!'

and

i will always

always

remember her.

one breath, one moment and i...
f
a
l
l
into the world

loathing as i do not having things planned, i still find
spontaneous moments have birthed my best days
like the afternoon in university when chris and i ran
through the rain
screaming out the poem from labyrinth together
or the night i went goth clubbing with timothy
and adam,
dressed in black and mourning the loss
of a good man.

or lazy, hazy summer days when i lay
in my hammock under the trees
dog beside me as the sun
beat down dappled through green
leaves.
these moments
not the big ones that come
with bass drums and whistles

but silent and sneaking pleasure for pleasure's sake.

we take the joy we're given

when we're given it

I stumble across you by the side of the road, legs
and neck at angles unnatural in both life and
death. The crows
have already been at your eyes, blank holes
staring at the sky as the sour smell fills the air around
making me choke on death itself. I remember
death I have seen: from the magpie
that lay below the blossoming tree with the scent
of funereal flowers, to the sheep in lamb
next door. I was a child, but I remember
my eldest brother

helping our neighbour, the crofter, trying
to save both ewe and lamb-in-breach—but
both dying, my brother hopping back over the fence,
arms soaked in birth-blood to his elbows, and I
buried my face in my mother's shoulder. Yet even then,
I knew that this was all a part of life.

I pass you again on my way home, holding
my breath. The flies have found you now, buzzing
around your corpse. This, too, is life.

Her smile is sweet, like the warm doughnuts she used to buy
when she was a student in the States, her Manchester tones
syrupy without being sickly. We share

our woes and follies, our foibles and little faults that have led us
here, to this clinical waiting room, this liminal space in the center
of a town I barely know. She speaks

of her partner, 'Bernard', but doesn't introduce herself, and nor
do I, but our shared brief cameraderie is enough for now,
for this moment in time. I tell

a story of previous experience, of trust and calm and eureka moments
in the strangest of incidences. She laughs, and sympathises, her hair
a perfect bob. It frames

her smile, bright and clear, and it warms me from the inside out, this
stranger-cum-momentary confidante. The dentist appears and calls for
Anita, and she leaves with a wave.

Strangers
pass like ships in the night
or like patients in a dentist waiting room,
apprehensive but cheering each other along.

What if our souls' colors were complementary, vivid blues and ocean
greens, would you love me then? The skin on the nape of
my neck aches for the press of your lips, soft skin damp with breath
                    pressing, pressing.
                                        What if
I wrapped the tendrils of my love around your fast-beating heart, not
squeezing but simply to hold you in an embrace within your chest,
pressing, pressing so lightly so as to let you understand
                                        I am there.
                                There is
            a path to tread before you love, but we
have worn the dirt down to stone apart, and together.

What if I chose to love you every day for the rest of my life. What if
                you chose me back.

        I yearn.
I yearn.
            I yearn.

the stories are true
or
      at least
            true enough—
       wronged women vilified for
    being
    wronged
        medusa
       assaulted and taken in a temple
       punished for her suffering because
       she dared to be a beautiful woman
    pandora
created to bring man's downfall
taught only deceit and destruction
punished for mere curiosity
              eve
          tempted by a snake to learn
          punished for mere curiosity which
          was already part of a bigger plan
      pasiphae
    humiliated by poseidon for
    her husband's sins; punished
    for taking her rightful revenge

a short list. the true list is
    longer
       so long it would not fit in all the books
       in all the libraries
       in all the world.
    women in history
         from the remembered to the long
           forgotten
           sisters in fate
         may we remember their truths
         and not men's lies.

Sometimes when I cry, I tilt
my head back to let the tears run sideways
tasting salt and bitterness in my
throat and on my tongue. I try
not to cry often, so tears come
at the strangest times, as though
they cannot wait any longer
to fall.

I cried easily as a child, emotions
brittle as butterfly wings as we caught
them in spring months, cabbage
whites and red admirals on bluebells
captured in sticky, childish fingers
as dust from their wings clung to
our skin. We knew then they were
fragile—

and of course we cared, but the lure
of the chase was irresistible. My
brothers showed me how, and I
enjoyed this connection. So much
older than me, they had little time
for a child, but this brought us
together for a fleeting moment.
Like salt

sea waves

drifting onto shore before they are
gone, again, and return, irrevocably
changed. Like salt tears, dripping
to the floor, drying so fast you never realize
they were even there.

Every night when the sky is clear I
look up, looking for
the stars and constellations I love and find
        a home in. I can

spot Alnitak wherever I am, on cloudless
nights, staring up until
my neck aches and I have to look back to
        earth again. I watch

the distant airplanes blinking their
way through the dark spaces
between the stars as though they are stars
        themselves. But last

night, as I watched the sky, the stars
seemed to move, gliding
quick toward the day-bright moon, and I became
        frightened. For the

first time, the dark night sky was a
source of fear instead
of comfort, as my brain wondered—enemy
        fighter jets? Or were

they alien spacecraft, positioning
themselves to conquer
our small planet? But then the sky righted
        itself and I saw

        I saw

the stars, locked in place as they
made their journey
across the night sky. And I, confused, knew
        I had dreamed myself

        awake

The power went out tonight. Only
for half an hour, I think, which is
nothing like when I was a child on
the island. Each year, winter would
come, and with it the storms that blew
around the house, taking down trees
and making greenhouses explode.
That happened to my parents, and
my mother, ever resourceful,
vacuumed up the shards with the old
cleaner.

The storms are still as bad, but
back then the power station was local,
and the lights would go out frequently,
usually for hours. When they did,
it was time to light the candles and
the oil lamps my parents kept for
just such occasions. We'd huddle
around the fire, playing board games (as
an aside, I hate Monopoly to this day)
or rummy.

These memories I have are fond, perhaps
because it was so frequent, a staple of
my childhood. It always seemed to happen
when there was something good on the
telly—I'm sure at least two different years
I only saw half of The Lion, the Witch, and
the Wardrobe. That was always shown
around Christmas in those days. That
makes me laugh—'in those days', as though
I'm eighty instead of only thirty seven years
old.

One year, by the light of the oil lamp, I sat
at the kitchen table, using my feather quill
and ink pot to write out song lyrics and
pretend I was a Victorian scribe, until
my fingers were smudged black. It took
a day to clear my ink-stained skin, but
the joy was worth it. I miss those days
in theory; in practice it's an inconvenience
to be without power now. Perhaps
what I miss is not caring, and finding
fun in simplicity.

I wish I'd had the confidence at twenty-five
that I have now, aged thirty-seven and some
months old. If I had known then what I know
now, as they say, perhaps…
but then, if things were different, I wouldn't
be the me I am now, with all my knowledge
and experiences. My life has shaped me
for the most part
to be kinder than I was a decade ago; kinder
to both others and myself. Would I have
the capacity for empathy that I feel within
had I not walked
barefoot through a hell of the wider world's
making? If the fires of fear and adversity
had not given me a deeper understanding
of my own pain
would I truly be able to comfort others
in theirs? Perhaps, after all, it is better
to have been forged by sorrow in the past
than sacrifice myself
in the present.

   (you fall one too many times
  and can no longer get up)
        (your heart is emp-
     ty, emp-
   athetic, emp-
  owered)
it goes like this:

  you cannot breathe in, only
      out and out and out, a time
   of panicked heart
 and
   panicked hurt
(it's like that)

   (begin at the end or
       end in the middle—what
  counts as beginnings or endings if you
       change the order
    of it?)

(but sometimes,
   sometimes,
     it starts like)

  a dark tree on the skyline
     the moon behind it, rising
   full and
  bright
 and with
     hope and love and joy, rising
     in your heart.

Everyone speaks about the roll of the dice, as though
this is the best part. It is
not. Unrolled dice are much more interesting. Potential,
not kinetic.

Many words have multiple meanings. Potential,
not kinetic. Once they are used, they are done.
discarded. The potential is
gone, replaced with something used. A paper tissue
in the trash.

Some people use more words than they need to as they
talk. Some people use far fewer. Neither is
wrong, but one leaves a greater
trail. Words spill, hitting the ground
almost audible in their dead weight.

To love a cloudless sky is to be dull. This
feels somehow like a
contradiction.

Your hair was naturally red—or so
my mother tells me. I just remember
you as a blonde. It made you look
more like my mum, your sisterbestfriend.
It's strange to think that years have passed
without you here—you who were always
so vibrant, even on days when your lupus
attacked each part of you. You were
so strong.

Stronger than your lupus.

But weaker than the cancer which took
you from us.

I will never forgive the doctors who failed
to look for the reason behind your pain
and instead blamed your illness. What if,
what if
            what if
                    they had caught it
when you first went to them. Perhaps
you would still be here—on the other side
of the phone, as we indulged wholeheartedly
in our mutual appreciation society. You
always called it that.

I just called it love.

When you knew there was no hope, you said
that you were having a happy death, with all
the phone calls and letters. I wish I could
be glad of that, but all I feel is anger that you
were taken from me
at all
and knowing you will never see me as I am
today, or know that I've achieved a dream
so long in the making
                        what good is success
        what good is it
what good is love when the ones you love
leave you.
Better to have loved and lost than never
loved at all or so they say. I suppose
it's true

but sometimes I wonder. Sometimes
in the dark of night when ghosts
wuther around the eaves
and I miss you so poignantly
I wonder if love is worth the pain.

But then, I remember your beautiful smile,
your laugh, your spirit, and I think—
perhaps
it's just one more reason to carry on.

If you could, would you read the last
page of the story of your life, just to
see how it ends? Would you take the book
in your eager hands, and flip through, seeing
births, deaths, and marriages until you reach
the end of your own story? Except, of course,
it is only the end of your story, your little arc
in the bigger story of the universe. I wonder
if you can even fathom how small the part
you have to play is. I know that I cannot.

And yet, although your story is one of billions,
you cannot call it insignificant. You hold
such potential within you, so much of a
possibility for kindness that can change the
world. You cannot even imagine the power
that you hold. If the universe is infinite, then
so are we all; we are all both infinitely small and
infinitely large. Both completely insignificant
but also unbelievably important. Infinity
stretches both ways, and you contain multitudes.

So when you have the choice to make,
choose kindness. It is the greatest power
you have.

It's not hard to find the shape of a heart
between her thighs. You say
you love her. Birds sing, they mate,
but love is not for birds. Or perhaps
it is.

A man searches the desert. He finds
sand, and an oasis. There is nothing
unusual. Except, perhaps, in a mirage.
Mirages are unusual, but so are what
they show. In the desert, water is
key. Perhaps this mirage shows water.
Perhaps my mirage shows love.

In the desert of life, you find
migraines and an oasis of calm
before the storms. Storms bring weather,
maybe a weatherman to tell you when they'll
stop. A weatherman is a metaphor.
The weather is a metaphor. For what?
Maybe your state of mind. Maybe your
state of love. Maybe the love you hold
for friends and family.

Maybe your oasis was the mirage all along.

My mother always told me I got it all from my grandparents—her
parents—a connection I treasured since I never knew my grandad
and barely knew my gran, too ravaged by dementia by the time I
was old enough to know her.
                            She was, by all accounts, an iron
fist in a velvet glove: kind but let no one walk over her (I aspire
to be the same, but it's hard in a world that tells you that if you
look a certain way you must be demure and polite and amenable
and submissive and also *nice*...)
                            But I digress, like I do, like my
mother always does too, easy distraction runs in the family,
but anyway, my gran was formidable but kind, but when I knew her—
or at least, the way I remember her—shrunken body in a special
home, unable to even *speak,*
                            only able to make purring
noises and unable to recognize her own youngest daughter, let alone
her youngest grandchild who had been born after the dementia had
taken hold of her mind. I remember my mother always took sweets—
malteasers, because they could
                            be sucked down to nothing (she had
long since lost her dentures)—but she like them, they made her smile,
and that made my mother cry. And the smell of the home and the old
lady with one empty eye socket and the discomfort and the sorrow—
they stick in my mind like burrs:
                            not happy memories. But important.
They're all I have of her other than the stories, and the fact my
mother believes I can sew and embroider because her father was a
tailor, and her mother was a seamstress, back in the day.

The snow falls, silencing the already quiet world
as we prepare for our yearly traditions. Christmas Day
is not the only day for traditions; the whole
holiday is filled with family and friends and *home home home*,
with all its joys and irritations. Robins
who sit outside waiting on food from my diligent
mother, and tweet, annoyed, if she's even a minute off schedule.

The stocking hangers still sit on the
mantelpiece, the decorations still in their places, waiting
for the twelfth day. Not superstition in this house.
Tradition.

Everything comes back to that. Fresh orange juice
and bacon rolls for breakfast, birthday cake
after dinner, then again for breakfast on Boxing Day,
no matter thirty eight years old. Sometimes
I think about our family traditions and wonder
how they look to outside people who hear
how rigidly kept they are.

Except sometimes they're not. Like last year
when I ate toast for Boxing Day breakfast instead
of cake. Except when my mother offers my niece's
French boyfriend cheese instead of birthday cake.

Tradition. A heavy word with heavy baggage. No one is free
if they are locked to tradition.
Tradition is habit with teeth.

The constant hum of air conditioning sounds
far too much like distant voices—perhaps
there is someone in the other end of the
large, open plan space with its modern, grey
-and-white-and-blue décor, its height adjustable
desks, its ergonomic black chairs. I could,
while here, completely alone, dance down the expanse
of floor; could race myself on the rolling desk chairs
from one end to the other.

In the end, I do none of these things. I sit
at my impersonal desk, screen casting its light
in my eyes. I work, and ignore the whispers
of the ghosts of corporations past.

The ship crashes through the waves;
the Blue Men are watching from beneath.
It sails on, unknowing, as Death strides closer.
Thunder rolls across the sky, nearly deafening
the sailors, soaked to skin as they
draw down the sails. The Blue Men
do not need to shout to be heard.
"faic thu fhèin a 'nochdadh
anns na tonnan fon t-soitheach[1]".
A panic goes around the deck, before
the captain takes his place at the port:
"mo mheòrachadh anns a 'mhuir
gu dearbh glè bhòidheach[2]".
The Blue Men frown, foiled this time
and Death retreats. No prize today.
The ship sails on to Ullapool,
sighing in relief, and the Minch calms.
She has no claim on them, for now.

---

[1] See yourself appear
in the waves under the vessel
[2] My reflection in the sea
is indeed very beautiful

The citrus fruits hang heavy, though they are still
too small. They drop, one by one, on the cold, hardwood floor.

It starts like this. You see the tree, but what you don't know is
the tree sees you too. They have
no eyes to see, no ears to hear, no
mouth to speak, and yet—
and yet—
somehow you hear them whisper. Their words
are lost in the wind.

Somewhere, in the distance, a gull cries.

She was
the first woman, first
of her kind, brought to life by Zeus as both blessing and curse
and given to Epimetheus, brother of Prometheus
in retaliation. Taught to weave by Athena and to speak by Hermes,
lies and deceit woven into the fabric of her. A box, a gift from
the father of all Gods,
went with her.

Yet we must begin at the beginning, when the world was still new,
and the Gods of Olympus were all powerful and known by man
to be kind or vengeful by turn. Prometheus, son of Iapetus, watched
as Zeus hid fire from man in punishment. His pity
extended to man and, against Zeus's wishes, stole fire back and returned it
to those who worshipped at the foot of the mountain. Zeus's anger
was known, then,

and Prometheus suffered a fate at his hands which reflected
the severity of his crime: to stay
chained
to a mountain, his liver eaten each day by an eagle, only to
regrow and be eaten again, for so long that Prometheus
may have forgotten how it was to live without pain. And yet,
before Heracles,
before salvation,
Zeus decided that this was not enough

and in his rage commanded that Hephaestus created from the earth

woman—

a woman: young and beautiful, both blessing and curse
to men, weak as Zeus found them. Hephaestus did
as he had been ordered, creating beauty from the filthy soil
and when she had been given life, Athena came.
Nameless as she was

she was taught to weave and create fine needlework by Athena,
until her arms ached and her pricked fingers bled red on the cloth
as she learned her craft. Once perfected, Aphrodite came down
and blessed her with grace and cursed her to bring

longing and cares, harsh and cruel, to the men of the earth. From Hermes,
the trickster God and messenger of Olympus,
she gained the power of speech; and when she spoke, Hermes taught her
to speak in artful lies and deceit, and she

not knowing better

spoke as she had been taught to do. Athena returned

and covered her nakedness in a silver gown. She
placed upon the woman's head a veil, embroidered by her own fair hands
with olive trees in flower to honor her. Persuasion and the Charites
came next, adorning her with such finery
as had rarely been seen off of Olympus; necklaces made
by Hephaestus himself, and a crown of polished silver atop her
auburn hair. Already heavy under the weight
of all the expectations and apparel,
the Horae set garlands of flowers upon her. At last

it was time for the final gift of creation: Hermes, smirking until the last,
named her Pandora, the "All-Gift", as she had
received gifts from so many of the Gods. And so complete,
Zeus deemed her ready.

He gave to her
a box,
beautifully and ornately carved from white poplar wood,
which he told her not to open, knowing
that the curiosity within her would be too great to bear. She
thanked him with a beatific smile
and took it, already wondering what was inside
but heeded his warning, and kept it shut. Prometheus
had warned his brother, Epimetheus, to not
accept gifts from the Gods, knowing Zeus's thirst for vengeance
would not be slaked by only one punishment. And yet,
when Epimetheus laid his eyes upon Pandora,

time

stopped.

Zeus offered her to him as his wife, and Epimetheus, being
only human, could not resist. Pandora's confused acceptance
of Zeus's will endeared her to him only more
and when he led her inside his home, she told him
only lies
as she had been taught
as had been instilled in her
as she had been created to do.

The box, now forgotten in the first rush of wifehood, yet still
sat beside the hearth. For days and weeks, as she discovered
the lusts of men and knew no shame from it,
it lay. But as with all, things must one day

change.

Epimetheus, called away by comrades to a night of revelry, left
his new wife alone. Pandora, alas for her, noticed again the box
and tentatively approached it. Picking it up, it did not rattle or feel
as though there were contents at all, light as it was. Atop the lid
was carved, in smallest detail, men bowing in front of a fire. As she
stared at it, the figures seemed to move, swaying as the fire flickered,
but when she blinked it was still once more. She knew

that she had been told to keep it closed and yet

and yet

what harm could it cause to merely crack open the lid? If indeed
something was inside, she would not let it out. In her confidence—
her hubris—
she cracked the lid

and
    out
        poured
          all
            sorrows
              and
                evils
              that
            men
          could
        ever
    have
known.

She cried out, wrapped as she was in the miasma, and tried in vain
to close the lid. But what she did not know, could not know, was
the will of Zeus cannot be defied. Finally
the lid snapped shut, and Pandora wept for the men of the world.

Just as she was close to losing herself to her
despair, the faintest sound tinkled from within. In fear
of what she might find, she forced open the lid, and out it flew:
tiny,
sparkling,
beautiful.
It whirled around her, and her spirits and heart lifted, for the speck
was hope. It followed the darkness of the world's evils, illuminating
all in its path, and men—affected as they were—could breathe once more.

For what
is life
without hope

but a faint echoing shadow of itself? She could not
reveal to her husband what she had done, and he
never asked why the box had disappeared from beside the hearth.

(Pandora, afraid still, had buried it in an olive grove and prayed that Zeus
was satisfied.)

She lived out her days then, as happy as she could make herself be, and lived
to see many women walk the earth, joining men as part of the populace

yet her secret remained with her until her deathbed. Before her last breath
she confessed her fault to her handmaiden who, once her mistress was gone,
wrote the story down as record. The tale
has been told for centuries, but few remember Pandora as she was:

created solely as a tool for vengeance, and forced to walk the path of her
destiny.

it always feels
like a warning
from the gods

when the sky falls into darkness
before the end of day
and light disappears, when

the world around you grays out
and nothing feels safe now
when

the world is gray inside of you
and nothing feels right now
it feels like a warning from the gods
a punishment for happiness

a feeling that permeates
the core
of you

like the scent of ozone in the field
like the wind picking up all-of-a-sudden
like crows wheeling in the air before a storm
like

your heart in your stomach

something terrible is coming.

Grief in Color

The women who flocked to your funeral were older, but
not as old as you had been. Many of them
had never met you. They knew you
by reputation alone, but that was
enough. One by one, they stepped up to the line,
shaking each hand with a murmured 'I'm so sorry'
or, 'I was in the rural. I heard so much about her'.

I think you would have been pleased, that your legacy
brought so many to see you off. But
my main memory of that day
is of the man who delivered your groceries. The way
he sobbed on my shoulder, uncontrollable storms
and floods. 'Sorry', he said at length, stepping back
and wiping his tears on the sleeve of his best black suit. 'Sorry'.

I wish you had known the depth of feelings
which people had for you, before you went
beyond. How we would grieve. I'm not sure
you realised how loved you were.

Somehow I don't think you would have believed it.

"They follow the boats, you know;
it's how you know the fish are plentiful."
So my grandfather told me as we stood
watching the gulls as they shrieked and cried,
wheeling above the waves. We stood
on that very pier every Saturday
waiting on the boats to dock;
waiting on the fresh fish.
It was always herring that he bought—
cooked in his smoker, we'd eat it
with boiled potatoes, using
our fingers. We never bothered
with cutlery in those days—we ate
that meal the way he had eaten with
his own grandfather, the way
all the old folks ate their smoked herring
and salted potatoes.
When he passed, at the ripe old age
of ninety one, I took my son
to the pier, and stood
watching the gulls. "You know
that fish are plentiful when
there are so many gulls," I said, hearing
my grandfather's spirit in my words.
"They follow the boats."

on my way home tonight, my booted feet
danced around the snails who had come out
after the afternoons rain,
                    trying not to crush
their fragile shells and destroy the life within
in my haste to hustle homeward to hearth and

warmth, sheltered from the oppressive sky
above.

i cannot guarantee that other travelers will be
as thoughtful, with heedless boots and bikes—
but to
         a creature whose life is so short
an extra hour might feel like an eternity
to live still, among the plants on which it
gorges itself to live.
                    and keep living.

we, all of us, merely want to keep living.

i

don't remember my first kiss. not who or how or
why but I remember practicing kissing

with

my friend's brothers, while she practiced
with the only boy hanging out she wasn't

related

to

and i don't

remember my last kiss. i guess
it must have been my ex saying

bye

at the airport but

but

i don't

i don't

remember. even though i feel

like i should.
*
it's such a personal thing—important
milestones to many. to me. and yet
my brain holds no recollection of
any of it. though i do remember

how d asked me out, on his knees in the back
of a blue mini, and kissed me
over the laps of the other girls
who squirmed and protested. in my yellow fleece.

memories are only strong chemicals and electrical
impulses. like a vhs they degrade, until nothing
is left but dust. history is written
by the victor. memories are written by our hearts—
and decaying synapses

The storm is a sou' wester, wuthering around the
stones, and I think:
    What does cause the random
   goose pimples—and why are they goose
   pimples?—that have no rhyme nor reason?
The wind does not reply, of course, merely
continues to howl softly
    (I secretly love the wind like this, and
   always pretend I'm a sorcerer, controlling
   the whirling leaves with my waving fingers)
On days like this, I think often about Death, as both
a being and a part of life
    (Not a terrifying figure but a dear
   old friend, a psychopomp who reminds you
   of someone that you knew but lost eons ago)
and although some call it morbid it isn't, really, just
another part of living things
    (Of energy, potential and kinetic, when
   nothing really dies, nothing really ends, but simply
   continues in a different form to the one you know)
It's normal to be fascinated. I think on my own mortality, on
what my last wishes would be
    (celebrate my life, buried or cremated?, cry
   only if you must but rather laugh and speak of the fun
   I had throughout my life, however long or short it will be)
Which brings me to the point: if I am cremated, then why do I
sometimes get a random shiver
    (in that strange way where there is no draft,
   there is no person behind you, that you know of, and
   someone always says the thing like it means something)
What is the significance of a goose? And why do you feel it
when it walks over your grave?

we waited for what felt like weeks for the eggs
                              to hatch, checking with
               the selfie stick held high
                              every day, thinking we
               could hear the babies
                              chirp. one day we went
          to the bench to enjoy the sunshine and there
on the ground
               was a broken egg
                    and we smiled
                              until the next time we were
                    out
          and there the chick lay
                    already starting to rot. i
would have cried, its tiny
               broken body at unnatural angles
                                   but we thought
                                   oh well
               there are two others
               and yet
          the next day
               we saw on the ground below the nest
                    two broken eggs
                         two broken bodies
                              and the third egg
          would never hatch
          since it was
never incubated.
                         do pigeons mourn their dead? do they
                              cry out somehow
                         when nature takes their offspring
          or is it
simply life
to them—
          raw and
               uncaring.

You and I lie like
Broken champagne bottles on the floor:
Cracked, shattered, empty.
Once we were whole, effervescent bubbles
Popping as we kissed.
Après moi, le déluge—but the waves
Have already come, spilling
Over us until we gasp for breath.
We tried, but failed
To make this last past its expiration—
Now everything about us is rotting,
Or decayed.
I stand and take a breath,
Pulling on clothes like armour,
And say goodbye one last time.

you do not gasp
                a breath
                        when you are told no
                        (expected or not)
                                        and it's fair
you do not cry
                salt tears
                        when you find out
                        (expected or not)
                                        the truth
you do not try
                to fly
                        when your wings
                        (expected or not)
                                        are clipped or
                                        Broken

                                        everything erodes

                                        everything falls

                                        everything—
                                        everyone—
                                        changes

~~you do not feel~~

you do not tell an artist to stop
                                making art

                                just because it makes you
                feel

Kindle me inside of you.
Set fire to my skin, my blood,
my bones within. Put your hands
around my heart to shield the flames.
The wind blows, the rain drives down,
but sheltered I burn from your spark.
The heat will warm us both
in these dull, cold autumn days
when darkness creeps and seeps
through every pore.
Strike the flint across the stone,
stand me above. Set me aflame
so I may fall to ash, and be reborn.

Your lips and fingers are stained purple-red from
the bramble bushes around my heart
the juice and blood from punctures mixing
in a painting far more beautiful than the old masters'.
You can try to reach through, pluck a single berry
but the thorns catch and scratch.

Sometimes I think you wish you could clear them away,
shear them away with sharp objects
yet you know that the danger of hitting the core is too great.
What you don't know is
every year you stay, they thin a little more;
the thorns less sharp, the branches less thick.
With every word you speak of
Love, of wonder, of beauty
the flowers blossom and die back to fruit.

There is a beauty in the pain.

It isn't the smell of the water, or at least,
you don't think so. It's more like
the hum of traffic, the "clackety-
clack" of the weaver next door. It
tastes like summer today, in the dead
of winter.

You don't, can't, won't know. Knowledge
is power, but there are earthy tones in ignorance.
Brown and green hues that sparkle in moonbright nights,
a glance from your window bringing,
if not comfort,
then something close by. It's
a robin on the tree, a phantom reflection. It's
something that tastes like defeat.

Moss grows on the side of your heart. This
is simply how life works. Your body is a tree.
But not at all like one. Trees are strong, hardy—
likely to fall in strong winds. Your body is
weak. And yet will withstand a storm.

The storm rages. The tree crushes your weak bones.
This is how life works.
This is how death weaves.

The first time we met in person you threw
yourself at me, and I, unprepared, still managed
to catch you and hold you close. You were
that sort, I remember; exuberant and full of life
even when you were too ill to walk. You would lie
with your head on my lap, as I played with your hair;
unwashed and slightly greasy under my fingertips, I
remember, but you
were still handsome.

I got the email where you told me you had fallen in love with me
while on the train home in December. I recall the feeling, hot
and cold all over all at once, because I was in love with you too.
It stung when things changed. I confess I was angry—not at you,
but at circumstances.

But I still loved you.

and I remember the day you died.

I have known my share of grief. To cry myself out at the losses I
have suffered. To write out my feelings, tears running on the ink stained
page. Yet for all that, I have never lost
the way I lost you.

we were no longer together.

but I still loved you.

I couldn't go to your funeral. Time and distance constrained me.
I sent flowers, a paltry show of my true feelings.

In December it will be ten years since we lost you.

You were a year older than me almost to the day, and yet
I am now nearly 9 years older than you ever got to be, and I think

I think

of all the things you would have loved in the intervening years;

but most of all

I think

of how

I miss you.

The day before Ash Wednesday—some call it Fat Tuesday, but
in Scotland we just called it Pancake Day. A day
where we gorge ourselves on buttery treats. In England,
of course
they eat crepes disguised with sugar and lemon juice,
but we ate drop scones in our house
with jam. I remember
one year at the school concert I performed a monologue
(ridiculous for a nine year old, but I always was
considered to be ridiculous
by my peers at least). The monologue
was three A4 pages long and I pored over it
for weeks before the concert.
(I still
forgot a little bit half way through; Mrs Morrison,
always on hand, prompted me with my line
and then I acted out the rest with my
usual gusto...
I've always had a flair for the dramatic)
I don't remember it now—flashes of a partial line
haunt me sometimes but
I remember the pride I had in myself
to have learned an entire monologue to perform.
It felt, to my young self, like flying, or dancing
in the skillet of life, sprinkling happiness like flour
over the floors.

Love and the Lies We Tell

He says he loves you when you ask.
He speaks and you, fool that you are,
believe him. It's easy to lie to yourself—
easier still to believe the lies of others.
Easier to accept the comforting false
than the terrifying truth.

Years pass. He says he never loved you
and your house of cards tumbles. He says
what you need can't be given. Your strength
crumbles into ruins. You believe the lie.
But this time it is the lie that hurts,
when the truth is:
you are deserving. You are not
impossible to love. It is merely
impossible for him to love you.

You think: perhaps he is right. You think
and your thoughts suffocate like smoke,
and just as insidious. The cancer is in your mind,
but no less dangerous. It eats away at you
and in the dark of the night the words
haunt you, their ghostly, poisonous whispers
in your ears. You cannot be loved.

No. He simply cannot love. A sad state, but
it is no more your fault than a falling star.
No more than the tide that washes away
the stone from the cliffs. It was
inevitable.

Stand up now and take a breath.

At thirty seven, she is not old, or so
she hears from friends, and yet
she thinks some days that her age
shows on her like patterns on a dress.
She goes to her garden and
        with an empty heart
tends to her flowers. Her neighbor
calls to her, and she smiles at him
although she cannot fathom a day
when smiling is not pain to her;
the womb which has never borne
        the child she craves
feels as though it sits outside
of her body, for all to see. Perhaps
it is lost among all the other patterns
of her life; the instruments she plays,
her country's flag, and the flowers
        from her beloved garden.
She cares for the flowers as she
would have cared for the child she
never carried. Poor substitutes,
yet they thrive under her gentle
care. She holds up her favorite pot
        with the face of a wolf
pressed to her own face and breaths in
the scent. Her heart and womb
are empty, but the flowers are in full
bloom. The lizard she fed as a child
with flies from her parents' garden
        is only a memory now;
it was a friend, a not-quite pet
and she sees its likeness now
as the gentle perfume wafts
in the evening breeze. She waves
at a mother and child on the street.
        Her heart is empty, but still
        aches.

It's not like we haven't
        been through this half a
    million times but you
          drag it up again, as you
             always want to do to win
             at any cost. You don't want
    to hurt me, or so you say, but the result
is the same each time.

"Let's make up" and I, as
        I am each time, am powerless
to resist you. You break me
    into more pieces than I could
          mend in this lifetime, even
          with all the glue and double
        -sided sticky tape. Blue Peter
    couldn't even help with us.

I don't want to fight. I never
    do, not with you, but you make
everything so difficult. Love
          may not be enough this time
      to mend us. "Kiss me" and
    I do. Even this hurts, you keep
        pins in your mouth to sweeten
your kiss. I'm addicted to the

    taste.

I do not want to drown in sorrow. I have known
love, and loss, with shocking intimacy; I have
wept—prone and barely able to catch a breath—on
a cold wooden hallway floor. I have grieved
both publicly and privately, tears shed in the harsh light
of my parents' bathroom before washing my face
and once the door is open again pretending
that nothing has happened.

To grieve is to gain a space in your heart which is never filled.
The love never leaves us, but its tapestry is now
interwoven with threads of pain and sorrow, as bright
as distant stars. Time and distance drain
the poison from the sting, still needle-sharp
even now. Old grief haunts our minds in odd moments
like the scent of dying honeysuckle lingers
on warm summer afternoons.

Loss is only the beginning of grief's journey, lasting
until we ourselves are gone, and then it is for others
to begin the process anew.

    The marshmallow cider I bought one
hot summer's day was somehow, at
the same time,
    both disgusting and delicious,
which frankly is somehow a metaphor
for life, and its ridiculousness. It was
a strange sensation to be both ends
of a very extreme spectrum simul-
taneously,
    but I'm not alone because
    it happened to Zoey too
when zie was drinking a bottle of
French vanilla coffee soda
and zie said exactly the same thing
about it, and I said, excitedly, "I
know what you mean!" and we began
ruminating on life
    and how we live both
        disgustingly, and
        deliciously,
at once.

"You're so sharp
you'll cut yourself one day"
blood on the knife of words
which sever and skewer others
and myself. A new knife, bought
to replace old. Sharp, too sharp.
Chopping apples for jam. The knife
slips. Blood
on white apple flesh. Blood
on white finger flesh. Blood
on white chopping board and
silver blade.

You're so sharp

you're so sharp

too sharp.

It's the crisp air that seems to burn your nose on
every inhale, the wind
so lazy
blowing through you rather than around as you
duck your head against it, pulling
your coat tighter
but it's never enough—the chill seeps
into your soul

this all sounds negative and yet
it's hot drinks inside as the weather rages
outside the windows
and the dark creeps into the corners of the world, the light
inside keeping the shadows at bay
and it's cosy sweaters
and children laughing in costumes
and spooky lanterns

it's golden leaves on the ground that seem to glow
even on the dullest day, bright
on your dark-sensitive retinas
kicking them up if they're dry enough, then looking around
to see if anyone noticed you acting
like a child
it's the turning point in the cycle of
death and rebirth, where the world scrubs itself
clean of the old
to ready for the new

it's the welcoming of the other side into your home
and heart
and hearth

whether you want to or not

When my great uncle John died, I went with my parents
to look through his things, to take mementos or
family heirlooms before his executor cleared out
the house. I took
his ancient Polaroid camera, knowing
that I would never get any film for it, but I remembered
him photographing me standing in front of the house
when my great aunt Nellie was
still alive. They
had never had children of their own, but loved me like
a grandchild. It felt
right, to take it, and as we looked through the photographs
we found, there were so many memories; I learned
who they had been through those photographs of family
and holidays. Nellie on
a beach, sipping beer from a bottle, or John digging the
potatoes with my father as a lad, or the waves
hitting the rocks next to an unknown lighthouse, the photo
edges ragged and discolored, the photograph itself
blurry with age and my great uncle's shaky hand—all of them
highlights of lives well lived
and loved
and cherished
blooming through the lens of my grief

Perhaps, if we had listened
more closely to the turtles, we would
have known they were not silent. Perhaps,
if we were not
so caught up in trying to be human
we would have known—we would
have known that speech is not ours alone,
would have discovered the way turtles speak to
one another sooner. Communication
is so important, and even they

even they

will talk with each other. I wish
I could speak turtle
or frog
or bee

If I were privy to their conversations
maybe I would truly understand what it means
to be part of a world
that lives and breathes so far outside
of narrow human experience
and learn from them the peace
of existing at one with the Earth.

About the Author

Joanna M. Lawrie is a Scottish author, currently living in the Midlands of England with Jimmy the Cat and too many books. Her main goal in life is to one day get enough sleep, and she hopes in the future to live in a house by the sea with many more cats and books.

Acknowledgements

This book would never have existed without the following people. Ria, whose constant support and kindness live in my heart. Rae, for invaluable encouragement. My parents, who have read each poem since childhood with enthusiasm. Adeline, Meg, and Bea for their kind feedback. Eve, for your help and advice on the cover art. You, the reader, for picking up my little book. Everyone who has ever given me kind words after reading a poem, who stood behind me when I decided to publish this book, who cheered me on in my darkest moments: thank you. Thank you. Thank you.